Darling Hedgehog Goes Down a Foxhole

Auralee Arkinsly

Illustrations by Julia Swezy

Library of Congress Control Number: 2019910962
Illustrated Early Reader Chapter Book, Fiction, Grades 1 & 2, gifted and talented.

JUV002110 JUVENILE FICTION / Animals / Foxes
JUV002180 JUVENILE FICTION / Animals / Mice, Hamsters, Guinea Pigs, etc.
JUV008050 JUVENILE FICTION / Comics & Graphic Novels /
JUV009040 JUVENILE FICTION / Concepts / Opposites
JUV018000 JUVENILE FICTION / Horror
JUV013060 JUVENILE FICTION / Family / Parents

To LuLu, Tristan, Jack Jack, and Joe-Joe

Chapter One

Darling the Hedgehog tripped. She tumbled down a foxhole. **WHOOSH!**

She rolled through the tunnel until she popped out into broad daylight at the other end.

PLOP!

Darling noticed the bushy tail first.

Miss Fox was enjoying a savory breakfast
on her back porch.

"Why *hello*, Dumpling!" said the fox,
putting down her knife and fork.

"My name is actually Darling," squeaked the hedgehog, "and I do apologize for disrupting your meal, but I'm looking for my parents. I saw them waddling together yesterday at sunset. Then they dropped out of sight!"

"Since they were still gone this morning," she continued, "I decided to track their footprints. Somehow, I fell into a foxhole and rolled all the way here!"

She glanced around at the strange surroundings. "Have you seen two hedgehogs by chance?"

The fox stood and appeared thoughtful. She then whisked past Darling and poked her nose into the foxhole.

"Why, no, Dumpling. But why don't you stay awhile and rest?" Beautiful Miss Fox glided into her back door and soon returned with something pink and puffy.

"Look what I have! It's a pink tutu and matching bow that's just your size!"

Curiosity won—Darling decided to try it on.

She donned the flouncy tutu. It was scratchy. It stuck out all around her middle. She looked like a pin cushion with a flair. Darling forgot all about tracking her parents.

She tried to look behind herself, but she could not see beyond the width of the tutu.

"You are so cute, Dumpling! I simply *adore* you," said Miss Fox.

"Why don't you tie this little bow onto that wonderful furry head of yours?"

"I have the same wonderful fur all over me!" Darling squeaked. She wondered silently, *why does she keep calling me 'Dumpling'?*

"Thank you, Miss Fox," she said after awhile, "but I haven't done anything special to deserve a gift."

"Oh, don't worry about doing anything special, little Dumpling," replied Miss Fox who had dressed herself up a bit. "All girls like pretty things."

"Still," said Darling, "there must be something nice I can do to repay you for these pretty things!"

"You don't have to do anything, Dumpling. I am just enjoying how adorable you are!"

"But, when I grow out of this tutu, you might not think I'm cute anymore." Darling became anxious that Miss Fox's adoration might just run out.

"So," she continued, "I'd like to find out what I'm good at to make you proud. But, I'm not sure what that is. What could I do?"

"Just sit there and look cute for me." Miss Fox sat down to let her breakfast digest.

"Nooooo!" cried Darling. "I will think a bit and come up with something better than *that*. By the way, Miss Fox, what are YOU meant to do?"

"Me?" asked Miss Fox. "Other than dressing up? I haven't thought much about that."

She took up her dishes, moved through the back screen door, and deposited them into her kitchen sink.

Darling called from outside the door, "Could you give me a little hint?" she squeaked. "Or at least tell me what makes you happy?"

Miss Fox thought as she rinsed her breakfast plate in the soapy water.

Returning, Miss Fox said, "Well, I do relish eating Sushi short ribs!" She licked her lips at the thought.

"And, I very much like to ride my bike...

...and, I play fence hopping with my friends."

"Are these things that I might do, too?" Darling thought about how fun it would be to pedal a bicycle up a rose petal path.

"I'd like that! Maybe my legs will grow long enough to reach the pedals and then I can peddle mushrooms in town!"

"I doubt that will happen," said Miss Fox as she considered the alternatives. "I've never seen a hedgehog ride a bike, but maybe I could carry you along in my pack."

Darling dreamed. "I can just feel the wind on my face!"

"While in my backpack?" Miss Fox asked.

"Here's an idea," she continued, "You'd feel the wind in my convertible! I could give you a ride. I'll hang you from a leather strap tied to my rear-view mirror so you wouldn't blow away."

So, Darling Hedgehog let Miss Fox tie a leather strap around her middle. She felt a tad bit nervous as the fox started the car and the wind began to sweep her off her feet.

Traveling with Miss Fox was more than a little bruising.

Darling swayed back and forth, bumping into the car and dangling dangerously as Miss Fox sped down the road.

Although she did feel the wind in her face, Darling had to catch the tutu before it blew away.

"There must be something else I can do... something I will like to do, *and* something that you will also like because I want to be able to thank you, Miss Fox."

"Well, you are quite round," said Miss Fox trying to be helpful. "I think you could be a *very* useful doorstop."

Though Darling's shape was more oblong than round, she thought it best not to correct Miss Fox. Instead, she said, "A doorstop? What's that?"

"I'll show you," said Miss Fox. She and Darling headed towards the herb and oil shop.

Chapter Two

Darling stood faithfully at the edge of the shop door all day, trying to be the perfect doorstop. Visitors came and went. A couple little ones tottered by the plump hedgehog and peered down at her with wide eyes.

"I don't think I like being a doorstop, Miss Fox."

The fox huffed, "Well, why must you do anything at all?"

"I want to do something I'm made for—something useful, something I enjoy doing and that you would like me to do for you. I want to give you something special, Miss Fox."

"Why, my little Dumpling?"

Darling reached out to hug Miss Fox. "Because you have been so kind to me."

"Oh, well..." Miss Fox patted Darling.

"But," Darling continued, "if I tried to cook your food, I would need a lot of help."

"And, if I tried to wash your dishes I would need a tall step stool. Oh, there must be something useful I can do!"

Miss Fox and Darling Hedgehog eyed each other.
All of a sudden, it felt awkward trying to be friends.

It crossed Darling's mind that maybe a friendship
with Miss Fox was not meant to be.

Darling's stomach suddenly made a noisy growl. "All of this thinking has made me very hungry," she said. "Do you have any snacks? Like maybe some yummy slugs?"

"Yuk!" scowled Miss Fox. "I hate slugs. They give me gas, and they eat my garden!"

Darling thought for a moment. "Hmm...so you say you don't like slugs?"

"Right." The look of distaste on Miss Fox's face made it clear.

Darling almost jumped out of her tutu as she squeaked, "I LOVE slugs! I can help you get rid of them!" She was more than happy to volunteer to eat Miss Fox's slugs.

"Well," said Miss Fox, "do I have to fry them?"

"Oh no, ma'am! I like them raw! I'll go get some right now!" Darling could hardly wait to start helping out.

"Why, thank you, Darling! That works for me!"

With each mouthful, Darling gained hope
that maybe she and Miss Fox could be friends.

"What about baby snakes, Miss Fox? I like those too!" Without waiting for an answer, she peered over by the shed to find several slithery snakes.

Darling snorted and grunted with glee as she ran off the porch and rolled down the steps into Miss Fox's garden.

"Do you like spiders, and bugs, and worms and mosquitoes?" asked Miss Fox.

"Oh yes!" Darling replied, "I eat mosquitoes as appetizers and worms for dessert! I'm definitely not a picky eater."

"I think we've found something that you like to do
that also makes me proud of you, Dumpling, uh, I
mean *Darling*," said Miss Fox. "What a big help!"

Darling's mouth was full, and she drooled a little
as she twirled and grinned at her new friend.

Miss Fox noticed the dumpling of a tummy growing
on Darling. She grinned too.

Darling stopped dancing. "Where's your dinner, Miss Fox?" She took her friend's paw and led her to the table on the back porch. "Why don't you sit here and I'll bring you something to eat?"

It had been a long day! Miss Fox sat down at the table and waited to see what Darling would bring her to eat.

Chapter Three

Darling ran inside the house to root out some dinner from Miss Fox's pantry. The back door swung shut behind her.

She stopped in her tracks, letting her eyes adjust to the dim light of the kitchen.

Darling saw cages of small animals and birds on the shelf. Then, for the first time in her whole life, the spines on her back shot up and stood on end. Her friend's pantry held a terrible sight.

"Oh, Miss Fox!" Darling said under her breath. She could hardly believe what she saw. As soon as she came to her senses, she quickly unlatched the cages and released the frightened animals.

Suddenly, a familiar voice called out, "Darling! Quit futzing around! We're right here!"

Looking up, Darling spied two roly poly shapes with spines standing on end—just like her own! There stood her parents trapped helplessly behind chicken wire. Frantic, they reached for their daughter.

"I can't believe my eyes!" Darling squeaked as she climbed the shelf and tugged at the cage door. It creaked open. They all leaped out into a hedgehog free fall!

They skedaddled for the front door as fast as their tiny feet hit the ground.

Unfortunately, Miss Fox's front door was closed tight. But, a window beside the door was parted just enough to let a cool breeze in—and to let the family of frightened hedgehogs out!

They tumbled over the windowsill and down to the soft grass. Skedaddle they did, as fast as their little hedgehog legs could take them!

When they finally arrived at their cozy nest, Darling pulled the bow hastily off of her head and began to cry. "I missed you, Mama and Papa! How could I have been so *wrong* about Miss Fox?"

"Don't worry, Darling," Mama replied. "Foxes are tricky ones! Have you ever heard the phrase, 'Sly as a fox?' Anyway, she couldn't have eaten us. Our spines would've pricked her tongue! But, we might have starved to death waiting to be set free."

Darling remembered that Miss Fox had tried to be kind to her, but Miss Fox is a *fox,* and it's in a fox's nature to eat small animals for dinner!

Mama hugged her Darling close. "Our darling daughter...our HERO."

"Darling to the rescue!" proud Papa agreed.

"I wonder if Miss Fox is still waiting for her meal..." grunted Darling.

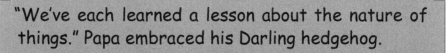

"We've each learned a lesson about the nature of things." Papa embraced his Darling hedgehog.

"Not every stranger can be a friend," he continued. "That is why we hedgehogs have prickly spines. They protect us."

Very soon, the hungry hedgehogs were grunting happily while hunting for a meal.

They were glad to have found their spines... and each other.

Thank you, Kathryn Swezy,
Sue Summers, Drema Shamblin,
Paula Freeman, Kathy Larkins,
Chelsea Bezuidenhout for believing
in this book enough to make good
suggestions with an eye and ear
to serve the minds of those special
first, second, and third graders.

-Auralee Arkinsly

The highest compliment to an author,
editor, and illustrator is a book review.
Thank you for sharing this story with
others and for your recommendation.

Check out our other books at
BooksForBondingHearts.com or
CaptureMeBooks.com

CAPTURE BOOKS

BOOKS FOR BONDING HEARTS

CPSIA information can be obtained
at www.ICGtesting.com
Printed in the USA
BVHW020610211019
561601BV00003B/66/P